Love Letters to my Babies
A Mother's Love in Words

Brittany J. Horn

Love Letters to my Babies: A Mother's Love in Words
Brittany J. Horn
Copyright © 2021 by Brittany Horn
ISBN: 9781736745526
All rights reserved. No part of this publication may be reproduced, distributed, or transmitted in any form or by any means, including photocopying, recording, or other electronic or mechanical methods, without the prior written permission of the publisher, except certain other noncommercial uses permitted by copyright law. All quotes are cited within the content, reference by the author, or are unknown and are not being credited to the work of any contributing author of this book. No portion of this work is meant to defame anyone but is based on my personal life experiences.
Edited by One2Mpower Publishing
Cover Design by Design Place
Published by One2Mpower Publishing LLC

Introduction

Being a mother and a wife was always my dream as a little girl. Out of all of my friends, I was the one who knew exactly what I wanted from the time I was a young girl.

God has definitely answered my prayers; blessing me to become a wife and a mother of five beautiful children. These weren't my only dreams but, definitely two of the things that were very close to my heart. One of my biggest fears was to fail as a mother. My plan was to be the best role model and mother ever but, life laughed at me and I ended up being the "Madea" of mothers.

I have always believed that children should grow up with their mother and father. So, stubbornly I only focused on that aspect of the belief. Unfortunately, holding on so tightly to that belief resulted in divorce and having to rebuild myself again. I had no idea that this would be the result but, hindsight is 20/20.

Let me truly apologize for the things you all were exposed to. I apologize for my all of my unhealthy behaviors and mindsets. There were some in which I was completely unaware of! Do not misunderstand me, if it's your goal to marry and have children, then yes, make it work out for the long haul! I fully support you, just be sure that the commitment is not to the detriment of yourself and others around you.

I want you to know that it's ok to let go and move on! I promise you that God will always provide everything you need. Family and friends are not exempt from "letting go"!

I've been through my fair share of pain and abuse in every

area! Mental, physical, emotional, spiritual, and financial! It wasn't just from one person either! However, I'm coming from victim to victor. I'm still here, glory be to God! I don't choose to carry the pain, only the lessons babies. That's it. Let it or them go! Just know that I am writing from experience.

I've lost myself so many times because I was more afraid of losing friends, cousins, siblings etc. I spent this part of my life not wanting to upset people and not causing people to be mad at me. "People pleasing!" But I was losing myself in the process.

Fear is a paralyzing emotion! I struggled with it as a kid, and it has followed me into my adult life, to be addressed head on. What you don't address as a child will certainly come up again in your life later.

I guess I can sum it up to not wanting to be lonely or alone and that's why I've held on so long to things. As I grow, I understand that there is a big difference between the two! Just because you are alone doesn't mean that you are lonely. I also know that you can be lonely surrounded by people.

More importantly, do not allow yourself to stay around people who make you second guess yourself. Do not stay around anyone who make you feel bad or uncomfortable about your dreams, goals, or desires. Most importantly don't you dare stay around anyone who does not respect the boundaries that you have put up to make you feel safe inside your own self!

I've learned in my past to never put my hands on anyone unless you are defending yourself. At the same time, never ever let anyone put their hands on you.

There is nothing that warrants that type of behavior. No one deserves that, period! Leave those situations that make you feel rage or subject you to abuse.

Moving away from those situations does not make you weak or a quitter. On the contrary it exemplifies your inner strength, self-control, and self-respect. In fact, it also preserves your self-esteem as an individual.

Love and respect yourself enough to stay grounded no matter what. Remove yourself from those who cannot honor you. The only chastisement you receive should come from your parents, grandparents, aunts, uncles, teachers etc. And honestly, there are limits to that as well!

In this life I have found myself giving more love and energy to others than I have given to myself.

This was due to a lack of personal boundaries.

Failing to honor myself, allowed all things to spiral out of control. I believed the thoughts and opinions of others should dominate my life. No more! Depression made me mean, mad, lazy, sad, and bitter! Ugh! There is a myriad of other things that could have destroyed all of our lives due to the way I handled or failed to handle my need to keep everyone happy.

I was fully aware that I needed help, I sought it out and received it. Unfortunately, I couldn't heal in the environment that I found myself in. I had no choice but to step away from everything that I had believed to be true. In doing so, I found out who I truly am and how to get to the bottom of what was hurting me.

It's so important to learn and know yourself to find your divine purpose. It is equally important to heal once you have figured out some of your own toxic patterns. Sometimes, healing requires more than prayer babies. Get help, especially when you find yourself going in cycles. There are things that you cannot face alone.

    I may not be able to give you everything financially right now but, I promise to give you my love and my knowledge. My unconditional love for you all is truly a divine gift from God. Loving you and giving you my best is my passion and purpose in this life! Not my only purpose but my greatest one.

    I wish that I could stay home with you all day! I wrote these letters to you all in my spare time, which is very rare for me to have so, please know that this is my passion project to you all. My deepest desire is to be free from work obligations and be a full-time stay at home mom.

I was broken, defeated, and discouraged, to be honest. But God! I had to remember who and whose I was, and that God makes no mistakes. I want you all to know that I love being your mother more than anything in this world! Being y'all mama is lit!! Lol!

To my Daughters

Never compare yourself to other women including your sisters! Ever!! Comparison is the thief of joy. Each and every person is unique, so there is nothing to compare. You don't compete where you don't compare. There is enough of everything for everybody!

    Be sure to uplift other women, even if they hate on you! It's ok to be loving, caring, kind and beautiful. Vulnerability is freedom and it's the most authentic thing you can be. Don't be vain but know that you are everything and be proud of who and who's you are! After all, Jesus thought you were to die for! Period!

    It is perfectly okay to shine bright and love yourself unapologetically. If someone doesn't like it, that is not your problem. Get far away from those types of people. Your only job is to work on yourself, get better every day, in every way!

Don't you dare carry the opinions of others! Yuck, it's too heavy! Give it to God and stay cute as ever, queens. That is a burden that doesn't belong to you!

Listen ladies, self-respect, self-esteem, and self-love are essential parts of self-preservation and becoming whole as a woman. There is no way that you can have any healthy relationships, friendships, and, or partnerships without first being healthy yourself! Be whole ladies! You can literally declare, "I am made whole" and watch God work! Get out of his way and do not try to do the work for him, yourself.

Do something daily to feed your mind, body, soul, and spirit! It's essential to set healthy boundaries for yourself and others! It's actually a must or everything will come crashing down! You will be depleted if you fail to nurture every part of you consistently! You have to put yourself first and love yourself with the love of God! It sounds cliché but it is such a real thing!

Girls, I am in the process of healing and learning myself all over again! It's a continuous journey. You never "arrive" so keep going. I've been spending time alone, listening to God and letting him heal my hurts! If you lack confidence in any area of your life, allow God to come in and heal that!

Love,
Mommy

The Fab Five

Please, do not try to fill the void on your own with things like drugs, sex, overeating-or alcohol. These were some of my personal codependent habits. Be better than me please. There are plenty of other addictions you can pick up in order to cover your hurts. Honestly, those are just band-aids, a temporary fix to wounds that need permanent solutions.

    I know that you all think that I am so confident but, I have definitely had my fair shares of insecurities. Trust me! To be transparent though the only thing that gave me peace and clarity was establishing a relationship with God. Running only sends you spiraling further down the rabbit hole. No matter how much I ran, my issues followed me. That's why I need God!

Every day I allow God to show me my worthiness! Insecurities are most often caused by comparisons but, worthiness comes from within ladies. No one on the outside of you can make you feel valuable! You have to know you are worthy of love regardless of what you do or do not accomplish in your life.

Please always be kind to yourselves. Learn to be gentle and relax. It's also important to know that you don't have to explain yourself to anyone. Your choices are your own and so are the consequences. Make sure you consider all of the pro's and con's before making decisions and choices.

Talk to God because our thoughts are not His thoughts! Let Him direct you in the way that you should go. He never misses the mark!

My love for you all is truly unwavering. In loving myself, I have more for you all! Sometimes, I need alone time to gather myself but, do not think for one second that I don't love you. It's necessary for everyone to have alone time throughout each day. That time allows you to get in touch with yourself.

There is only one me and five of you so, cut me some slack my loves. I know that each one of you needs me in your own way, so I am always thinking of ways we can engage so that we can have one on one time. I am never going to be everything that you need in life, it wasn't designed that way! There will be some areas that I lack as a parent. Again, that's where God comes in.

Do not expect me to be a perfect person just because I hold the prestigious title of being your mom. Motherhood allows me the unique opportunity to be the student and the teacher at the same time.

As you grow up, there will be some things you'll feel that could have been handled differently. That's how life goes. Don't judge, just observe, and move accordingly. Do not let life make you bitter!

No human being can fulfill every part of you, they are not supposed to. That is codependency and it's unhealthy to expect that complete fulfillment from other individuals because each person is on their own personal journey.

I am still healing from things that happened in my childhood. I had two sets of amazing parents. They were not perfect but, I also understand that they did the best that they could with what they knew and had. For that I'm grateful. That's all you can ask of anyone.

Your relationship with the divine is key to this life. Life is unpredictable as we've seen and experienced firsthand. God is the only thing that's unchanging. He is my rock! In my 'Plies voices'! Lol!

Everything that I have sacrificed thus far has been worth it! You all are so worth it. It is my absolute goal to help you all become whole individuals before you leave my house. Daily I pray to protect you mentally, physically, emotionally, spiritually, and financially! My hope is that you all will be whole, highly functioning independent adults. Whole meaning: knowing, accepting, and loving yourselves completely.

It's crucial that you all understand you will never be perfect but, it's okay to strive to be the best you. Healing isn't comfortable, cute, or ideal but, healing is your responsibility.

Having faith is extremely important to have. Faith does not

make dealing with obstacles easier, but bearable. Faith also helps you establish the boundaries that you need to set for yourself and others.

My desire is for you all to stay open minded and be free thinkers. I cannot tell you what to believe in specifically but, I can most certainly testify that God has brought me through each and every trying situation I've faced. I may not have seen it in the process, but I know that He's been with me from day one. So. yea for me, it's Jesus for the win! That is not up for debate. We only answer to God!

Love,

Mommy

Bre'Jai D.

Poot, I love you so much! You are my big girl, my little gift and mommy's helper. My first born with my name sake. A creative name for my creative child. I gave you my first and middle name. Creating a name fit for a queen. You are the QB2 to my QB "Queen B." You are extremely talented. I want you to know that there is not one thing you can ever do to change my love for you. I love you deeply and completely. You are so intelligent that it often blows my mind. I wish that I could figure things out like you do with little to no effort. That is one of your greatest gifts. Your brain is amazing; use it for good things queen.

    You have such a deep understanding about so many different things it's unbelievable. It's okay to strive for the best in life, in fact I encourage that. Don't ever stop complimenting yourself on all your many accomplishments. You are great with or without straight A's. Do not worry yourself so much. Always focus on what matters most in life and that's LOVE. Love for yourself is the most important type. Love for God and others are also very important. Don't spend so much time trying to reach a goal that you forget to just enjoy being you. Go easy on yourself but stay focused at the same time. You are a magnificent person. You are absolutely beautiful inside and out. Such a fun and unique girl you are. You are and will always be a queen no matter what. No one can take your crown from you "QB2!"

    Don't get mad when others don't understand you. I told you that people don't deserve that much of your energy. Plus, most people barely understand themselves. I understand that people and things can disappoint and hurt you, but don't take it personally. Other people's perspectives are out of your control.

You have such a kind heart and so much compassion that it's disheartening when people do ugly things but remember who you are at all times. I know; and fully understand the heartache that disappointment can cause but, you also have to consider that everyone does not think like you. Allow People have different thoughts and beliefs. Be open minded and learn to let go and let God.

Watch your words when you are upset. You cannot take back your words and you never want to be the reason why someone is torn down. That's not how us queens operate. Remember you attract more bees with honey. You are unique, which means there is not one person in the whole universe that is like you.

People, including family, will try to take advantage of you but, it is essential that you set healthy boundaries to protect yourself from that. Do not give so much of yourself that you don't have anything left for yourself. That includes gifts, resources, help, time, and energy that you need to keep yourself afloat. If there is something that makes you feel uncomfortable deep in your soul, pay attention to that feeling and change your direction or the people causing you to feel this way.

Be your own person, and don't let anyone change you. It is perfectly okay to say no to others, without an explanation. God makes no mistakes and baby when He made you, He broke the mold. I'm sending kisses to my first daughter.

You are my first true unconditional love that made me a mother and a better person all together. I will love you forever Bre'Jai D'Vine Horn. I cannot wait to see what God is going to do with you! You have so many talents inside of you so, please use your talents wisely and use as many as you can. Love hard and forgive harder.

Always express yourself as much as possible and stay true to and go hard for yourself. Always pray! I am "happy at you!" as the twins would say! Lol!

Love,
Mommy Boo

Ri'Ane

My Moo, hey girl hey! My diva, my pretty, pretty smart, little mini me! You are just so bomb to me. You are so sweet and calm in spirit- sometimes! Lol! Your heart is so big, and you are "super" special to me for many reasons. You have no idea what you mean to me but, I'm writing this just to give you an idea.

When you were born, there was so much going on in my life at twenty years old. I promise you, when I saw you, you changed my whole dark heart. I want you to know that it is ok to be "weird", "strange", or whatever people refer to as different. Stay there, that's where all the good in life is. Never ever let anyone including myself keep you from being your expressive self.

I don't have to tell you to make sure people stay in their own lane, because you don't take any mess and have no problem putting people in their place. Period! However, at the same time, please work on directing your frustrations and anger toward positive things and not people. You don't have to be cruel to get your point across. I get it, sometimes people will take you there but do your best not to let them.

    Help me to teach your siblings the art of peace that you have mastered so beautifully. I really admire that about you. You are so chill and at peace with yourself, such a very gentle soul. There is power in your peace baby girl, don't you dare let anyone steal that from you because you are a powerful being. I love you so much, and I wish I could have more girl time with you just to hang and be cute. That's my favorite thing to do with you. I love when you tell me stories about what's been going on in your life, because it is important for me to know about you.

Keep being an example to others as you love and honor yourself. Don't go overboard with the vanity though "cuteness". With kind words and that loving peaceful heart, you will always win in life. Take life easy but always be true to Ri'Ane Chellise McIntyre. Mommy's fashionista, diva, helper, big sister, rapper, singer, beauty queen, my brownie, my "it" girl!

Love,

Super Mommy

Mckenna Royce

Mommy's pretty rainbow baby! Thank you Yachty, for saving my life! Singing your song to you, "Eeschlosh Kenna bomp, bomp!" My pretty little thang with the pretty eyes. Your little eyes tell so much about you Kenna. I want to tell you that I am sorry for not being able to give you more of me, "my time"! I am doing my best to be an individual and a mom at the same time.

      Being a mom of five is not an easy task but I will never give up on being your mommy, girl. I am fighting for you baby love. You are never left out of my heart or my mind, so never feel that way. You are my lovebug, baby girl, I just want to hug and kiss you all the time.

You are so sweet-natured and humble. I just love your spirit. You know that you're pretty, but you do not let it go to your head. You are not just beautiful on the outside though baby girl, please know that you are so much more than looks. You have a soul glow girl! I'm sorry that your sisters are sometimes mean to you, that is not ok but, please understand that they are working hard to help mom.

I'm doing my very best to work on having a much more loving household. I need you to work with your sisters though. Go easy on them, they have been through a lot. We are all doing our very best.

They get tired and frustrated when you are not listening, so remember to be a good listener. Don't believe everything that they tell you to scare you. Lol! Everything is not that serious baby. I love you so much Kenna so, with tears in my eyes, I ask that you forgive me if I don't hug and kiss you as much as you need.

Mommy is healing and working diligently on being a better mom and person. I promise things will get better for us soon. Life is so much more beautiful with you in it. You are so smart and clever and the best cleaner in the house.

You do a good job with keeping everything including yourself "so fresh and clean". You are such a great big sister and role model. You are my dance machine! I just love watching you dance, even when I'm tired and wore out from the day.

You bring the sunshine to the world baby girl. Don't let people take your kindness away. They will try but allow your beautiful heart to shine through and remember this; when people are mean to you, it has absolutely nothing to do with you. It is a direct reflection of that person. Don't take it personal even if it's a personal attack.

When you feel like someone isn't treating you right, get as far away from them as possible. Do what you have to do to keep that beautiful heart glowing. Mommy loves you pretty princess always, no matter what.

Love,

Mommy/Dance Partner

Kalib John

To my only son, my answered prayer, my honey love, my stink, my big man, my big dude, my sonny boy, boy! Son, the amount of love I have for you in my heart cannot possibly be expressed in words. You are a joy to all who encounter you.

    You are the coolest cat in town. You are so smooth, chill, handsome, gentle, and yet, so serious. You have truly changed the game son. What a true treasure you are. Son, you were well worth the wait. Everyone loves you stink, never forget that.

    You are far better than anything I ever imagined in my dreams. I dreamed and prayed for a boy for several years, and I thank God for blessing me with you. He gave me the cream of the crop when He blessed me with you. You son are proof that God really does answer prayers!

There is such a strong bond between a son and his mother. There will be nothing that will change my love for you son. Please always love and believe in yourself. Always strive to be the best man that you can be. I pray for you so much because it is not easy to be a man. I obviously cannot relate, but just know that I understand. You know, anyone who is in opposition of young black youth due to prejudice. So please be sure to stay ten toes down.

There is a direct attack on your power and manhood in general. Whenever your back is against the wall, always run to God. He is your strong tower. Remember, God is your unlimited source son. Seek God at all times in life; happy or sad.

I am not a man so I cannot tell you much about being a man. But I will show you how to love and respect yourself and others. I will uplift you at all times. I want the world for you son, and I hope that you realize your purpose and your place in the world.

Please develop and maintain a strong mind. If you need to talk to someone, don't you dare hesitate to reach out to me. If I, or any of other family members are not available; reach out to someone you trust. Please do! If you need to, do not hesitate to speak to a therapist.

There is no shame in asking for help so, do not ever suffer in silence!! It's a harsh world baby boy but, I need you to stay strong and gentle at the same time.

Pay attention to the world around you, watch your mouth, and actions! Don't let the world turn you into a monster. You hold the key to your future son, so use your time here on this earth wisely. You are powerful.

No one can take your power from you unless you give it up. Be expressive with your feelings but with limits. Don't be swept away by emotions to the point where it leads to anger outburst. It runs in the family so please be careful. Never ever put your hands on a woman, or anyone please, unless it's in self-defense. But there is so much strength in walking away.

Respect yourself enough to never let anyone put their hands on you either! I want you to value yourself and others. You will obviously be skilled in understanding women, so act accordingly. You have too many sisters to be manipulated by one or vice versa. It's ok to be vulnerable with the right person though.

Never let anyone walk all over you. You are not a doormat. Son, know that you are a king no matter what! If people don't treat you as such, move around. Don't cry every time something gets hard because there will be plenty of hard things in life. Look at the hard times as an opportunity to become a better person.

Your emotions and feelings are valid so never allow anyone cause you to doubt yourself. However, process them in a healthy way. I have so much more to say to you, but later. I love you Leo the lion, my pride, my joy. Be great my king.

Love,
Boobee, Mommy

Kali Alyse

My pretty Ta-Ta! Mommy's Leo queen, my sweetie cakes, my princess pooh! "Oh, my goodness" is the only thing I have to describe you. You are so much of everything Kali, just the total package!

You're my little free thinker, and such a free spirit. You're my little love in abundance. Mommy's beautiful little snuggle bunny. You're the boss lady, and so funny. I honestly had no idea that I could love one more girl in my home! Baby, when I tell you that God sent an angel to me through you, I mean it.

Mothering twins is no easy task, but baby girl, you make it all worth it! The love you give so effortlessly is a direct reflection of how God loves us! You are always in tune with everything going on around you. You just go with the flow baby doll and I love that about you.

Please don't ever stop believing in yourself. I am begging you to stay as free as you can. There is no better place in the world to be besides, being in tune with God's spirit! Reach for the stars, Tots. There's nothing in the world that can keep you from being everything you want but you! You are your own competition baby. Listen, I promise that you are me. It's like watching myself at your age!

People will be out to destroy your confidence. Confidence is one of the greatest gifts that we possess if we build on it. Our hearts are strong, and most people won't understand how you operate. Ignore anyone who doubts your abilities and keep following your dreams, Tots!

Kali Alyse McIntyre, no matter what happens in your life, do not let it turn your heart bitter. When you are gifted, there are forces set up for your downfall. Do not let anyone make you second guess yourself. However, take it from me, you don't have to learn everything the hard way.

    Always remember that you are amazing even when you're sitting down doing nothing. It's perfectly okay to be a lone wolf sometimes. Don't lose sight of your worth, you are a priceless sweet girl. You're generous, baby because your heart is gold. But don't let anyone take advantage of you and don't take advantage of others either.

    Don't let anyone tell you how to do you. You should however love yourself enough to have boundaries for yourself and others. You are not a possession, Tots! Do not cage yourself in your mind and don't allow anyone else to cage you in with their expectations either.

Baby girl, you are a shooting star. There are infinite possibilities for you. You are a ball of magic stardust power. You will encounter jealous spirits and people who are mean unnecessarily. Understand that they should be seen as tools to better yourself. Don't be mad at them, forgive and move on Tots.

Keep your heart and your intentions pure as much as you can. Pray always! I know that it will be hard at times but, remember that you are here for a purpose; to walk in Love. Most times you will not get the same amount of love back. Love them anyways and remember God's love will always be there. He always reciprocates what you put in. You do not always have to be right and it's okay to be quiet.

Wear your crown proudly and keep your head high. Dance that dance, sing that song, do whatever you do with joy and your whole heart! I love you for so many reasons, Tots. You are my girl; I hope we stay close forever. The Leo Lions stick together always. Plus, our birthdays are a day apart, so we are tied to each other. I'm always here for you baby pie! I am here for you to talk to at any time.

Love,
Mommy Lady

Please...

(P)lease (L)isten (E)xecute (A)sk (S)erve (E)xceed

I hope that you kids feel as blessed as I do to be a part of this crew! You kids are amazing! Watching you all grow every day is a joy. So much personality bursting out of all of you, and so many attitudes to deal with daily. I enjoy teaching you all every day. It's an honor to show you how to control yourselves in different ways.

Every one of you has your own special and unique gifts. Use them as much as you can and perfect them. Whenever you get down, tap into one of your many talents and create something new. Creating is what we were born to do!

I hope that the messages that I have shared will be of value to you at some point in your journey!

Thank you for all the love you give me daily. Each one of you, love me in spite of me.

You love me despite my shortcomings and imperfections. You even love me after being disciplined. Your love is truly unconditional! What's better than the love from your children? Well, God's love of course. But there is certainly a direct correlation between the two.

I feel so blessed to be mommy to my five little blessings to love and cherish daily. Know that I'm always here for you. Thanks for making our team great. We are all blessed, favored, and gifted!

Don't forget to stay grateful for everything, always. We work together as a unit and as long as you all remember that we can make it through anything. We are more than conquerors! God causes all things to work together for the good of those that love the Lord. God will never leave us or forsake us! Be encouraged because Jesus overcame the world.

Try your best not to complain, and never forget, "life is 10% what happens and 90% how we react to it!" So be quick to listen, slow to speak and quick to forgive! **Show up for yourself!** I'm sending a million kisses to all five of you! My love letters to my 4 ladies and my big man!

In conclusion, as you journey through life, I leave you these questions to ask yourselves. They are far more valuable than anything I could ever buy you! As you embark on your own personal adventures, please ask yourselves these questions and answer honestly for true results. The outcome will be a life of personal accountability and healthy living.

Below is a personal study guide with space for you to respond. This guide will also assist in navigating the storms of life. So be honest because you owe it to yourselves. I Love You All with everything in me, so please accept this token love from Mom.

Self-Study Guide

Who are you?

___

Are you comfortable with yourself?

___

What do you believe about yourself?

___

What do you love about yourself?

___

Are you open?

___

What do you want for yourself?

_____

_____

What steps can you take to make this happen?

_____

_____

Are you healed or working on becoming healed?

_____

_____

What are your struggles?

_____

_____

_____

What are your fears and insecurities?

_____

_____

What makes you weak?

_____

_____

Are you judgmental?

_____

_____

Are you your own worst enemy?

_____

_____

_____

_____

Do you have a healthy relationship with money?

_____

_____

Do you expect too much from others?

_____

_____

How do you handle let downs or disappointments?

_____

_____

What do you do in your free time?

_____

_____

How much time are you committing to your own personal growth?

_____

_____

Who is in your circle?

_____

_____

How well can you walk away from things that no longer serve you?

_____

_____

How committed are you to your own obligations?

_____

_____

_____

Do you spread yourself too thin trying to be and show up for everyone but yourself?

_____

_____

What are your spiritual practices?

_____

_____

How well are you sharing your gift?

_____

_____

Are you a worrier or a warrior?

_____

_____

_____

Does your belief hinder or help your growth?

Do you use your beliefs to build others or to tear them down?

How well do you actually get along with others?

Are you a control freak?

Are you able to go with the flow?

_____

_____

Do you enjoy your own company?

_____

_____

Do others enjoy your company?

_____

_____

What can you offer to yourself or another individual?

_____

_____

_____

Are you aware that you can't pour from an empty cup?

_____

_____

Do you know that you are enough?

_____

_____

Do you know that everything you seek is inside of you?

_____

_____

Do you know that you lack nothing?

_____

_____

_____

Are you an unconditional lover or do you have a strict set of demands?

_____

_____

What does love look like to you?

_____

_____

Do you expect too much from others?

_____

_____

Do you set boundaries?

_____

_____

_____

Do you have too many boundaries?

Do you crave the support and acceptance from others?

What do you do when you do not receive it from those you expect it from?

What thing in your life needs balance?

Are you the person that you want to attract?

Are you aware of the emotional triggers that can set you back? How well do you know your own voice?

Do you communicate effectively?

How in touch are you with your words and emotions?

Can you trust yourself with your secrets?

_____

_____

Can others trust you with their secrets?

_____

_____

Are you serious about your life and well-being?

_____

_____

Do you plan for the future?

_____

_____

_____

Do you allow space in your plans for things to change?

_____

_____

How well do you save your money?

_____

_____

Do you make enough money to manage household responsibilities?

_____

_____

Are you a safe place for someone to be freely open with you?

_____

_____

_____

Are you a team player?

___

Do you allow people too much freedom into your life?

___

Do you feel like you are always a victim?

___

Do you know how to take control over your life?

___

Do you take accountability for yourself?

_____

_____

Do you think before you act or are you led by emotion?

_____

_____

Are you a talker or a doer?

_____

_____

Do you have the ability to do both?

_____

_____

_____

Can you rebuild from destruction or do you need a whole new clean slate?

_____

_____

Do you know how to close your mouth?

_____

_____

Do you know when to speak up?

_____

_____

Are you willing to separate head and heart to live a life you are deserving to live?

_____

_____

www.ingramcontent.com/pod-product-compliance
Lightning Source LLC
Chambersburg PA
CBHW061507040426
42450CB00008B/1519